**Outside front cover:**
*(top left, and page 38)* Fair Buttons; *(top right, and page 21)* Plough Pudding; *(bottom left, and page 12)* Potted Crab; *(bottom right, and page 37)* Apple Johns and Biffins; *(background picture and opposite)* the Norfolk wherry has long been a symbol of the county.
**Outside back cover:**
*(top)* Cley-next-the-Sea; *(centre, and page 11)* Soused Herrings; *(bottom, and page 33)* Norfolk Syllabub.

In the same series:
*A Little Book of Scottish Recipes*
by Mary Norwak

Photography by John Brooks
© Jarrold Publishing 1999

ISBN 0-7117-1087-2
© Jarrold Publishing 1999
Designed and produced
by Jarrold Publishing, Norwich.
Printed in Spain. 1/99

*Nelson Slices (page 41)*

# A·TASTE·OF

# Norfolk

## A collection of regional recipes

*by Mary Norwak*

JARROLD
PUBLISHING

# INTRODUCTION

NORFOLK is a bountifully rich agricultural county, with great harvests from both sea and land. Because of its location, the county enjoyed a close relationship with the Low Countries, Germany and Scandinavia, and the wealth of the wool trade helped to build its churches and great houses, just as the herring trade of Great Yarmouth ensured prosperity for Norfolk's ports and fishermen. The good climate and soil gave farmers the chance to grow wheat and barley to produce essential bread and beer, and apples for local cider.

   With such wonderful produce, and a long history of prosperity until the end of the 19th century, the county built up a reputation for good, nourishing food. The dishes were simple but satisfying, displaying the fresh ingredients to their best advantage. The selection in this book comes from generations of seafarers and farmers and the thoughtful housewives who were able to record their family favourites.

*Cley-next-the-Sea*

# CONTENTS

# FISH

The range of fresh fish available in Norfolk is enormous. Great Yarmouth is famous for its herring and the tradition continues with smokehouses producing kippers and the Norfolk bloater. There is also a wonderful selection of shellfish, from Cromer crabs to Sheringham lobsters, whelks of Wells and shrimps of King's Lynn.

## SEA PIE

### SERVES 4

*1 lb (450g) cod fillet*
*1/2 pint (300ml) medium cider*
*1 lb (450g) cooked potatoes*
*salt and pepper*
*a little milk*
*1 oz (25g) butter*
*1 oz (25g) plain flour*
*2 large tomatoes*
*2 oz (50g) grated cheese*

Cut the cod into cubes and put into a pan with the cider. Cover and simmer for 20 minutes. Drain the fish, keeping the cooking-liquid. Put the fish into a pie-dish. Mash the potatoes well with milk, salt and pepper, and spoon into a border round the fish.

Melt the butter, stir in the flour and cook for 1 minute. Gradually add the cooking-liquid and bring to the boil, stirring well. Season with salt and pepper and pour over the fish. Slice the tomatoes across and arrange on the top, then sprinkle with grated cheese. Brown under the grill and serve at once.

Cider is used in many Norfolk recipes since it was made in large quantities in the county. Here it is combined with sparkling-fresh cod in an unusual pie without pastry. The tomatoes have only been included in the last 100 years, but may be omitted if not liked.

9

Soused Herrings

# Soused Herrings

**SERVES 6**

*6 herrings*
*salt and pepper*
*1/4 pint (150ml) malt vinegar*
*1/4 pint (150ml) water*
*1 tablespoon pickling spice*
*3 bay leaves*
*1 medium onion*

Clean the herrings, bone them and discard heads and tails. Sprinkle with salt and pepper, and roll up with skin outwards. Place close together in an ovenware dish. Add vinegar and water, spice and bay leaves. Slice onion thinly and place on fish. Cover and bake at 150°C/300°F/Gas Mark 2 for 1 1/2 hours. Serve cold with brown bread and butter. If preferred, use dry cider in place of vinegar and water. The fish will keep in a refrigerator for up to 5 days.

Great Yarmouth became famous for its herrings when the eating of fish was compulsory on many days for religious reasons, and the fish was salted and exported all over Europe. The Great Yarmouth Herring Fair lasted for 40 days and was first held in 1270, continuing well into the 18th century. When Norwich was an estuary fishing station, the city had to make an annual delivery of 24 herring pies to the royal court. At home, herrings were 'soused' in vinegar, cider or beer as this preserved them for a few days.

**11**

Norfolk people and their visitors look forward to a summer treat of fresh Cromer crab salad or sandwiches. Thousands of crabs are brought in on the boats, and many people are employed on the tedious job of boiling and dressing them. This is a delicious way of serving crab as a snack or the first course of a meal.

Herrings and mustard are both famous Norfolk products. Here they are combined in an easy but tasty dish. The mustard offsets the oiliness of the fish, and the oven-baking reduces the strong smell of cooking.

# POTTED CRAB

### SERVES 4

*4 oz (100g) butter*
*¹/₂ teaspoon pepper*
*¹/₂ teaspoon ground mace*
*pinch of Cayenne pepper*
*8 oz (225g) crabmeat*
*juice of ¹/₂ lemon*

Heat 1 oz (25g) butter and add pepper, mace and Cayenne pepper. Stir in crabmeat and lemon juice and stir over low heat until the crabmeat is hot but not brown. Spoon into 4 individual dishes, and press down lightly. Leave until cold.

Melt the remaining butter and pour into a bowl, leaving the milky solids behind. Pour the butter over the crab and leave until cold. Serve with hot toast and lemon wedges.

# HERRINGS WITH MUSTARD BUTTER

### SERVES 4

*4 medium herrings*
*3 oz (75g) butter*
*1 teaspoon mustard powder*
*salt and pepper*

Preheat oven to 190°C/375°F/Gas Mark 5. Clean and fillet the herrings and open them out flat. Cream the butter with the mustard, salt and pepper and spread on the open fish. Fold in half and wrap each fish in a piece of kitchen foil. Put on a baking-sheet and bake for 15 minutes. Serve hot with boiled floury potatoes, or with brown bread and butter.

*Potted Crab*

Oysters were very cheap at the beginning of the 19th century, and this was a typical dish for a light supper. This recipe was given by Mrs Dashwood to her friend Mrs Gordon, a Norfolk rector's wife, about 1820.

# OYSTER LOAVES

**SERVES 4**

*4 bread rolls*
*12 oysters*
*1/4 pint (150ml) dry white wine*
*pinch of ground mace*
*pinch of grated nutmeg*
*freshly ground black pepper*
*1/2 oz (15g) butter*
*1/2 oz (15g) plain flour*
*3 tablespoons melted butter*

Cut the tops from the rolls and keep on one side. Scoop out most of the centres, leaving a 'wall' round each roll to serve as a container (use the breadcrumbs for another purpose). Open the oysters and put them into a thick pan with their liquor. Add the wine and seasoning, and heat gently until warmed through.

Mix the butter and flour together and stir into the liquid. Stir over low heat until the liquid has thickened. Place the rolls on a fireproof serving-dish and fill with the oysters and sauce. Replace the lids and pour over the melted butter. Put under a medium grill just long enough to make the tops crisp, and serve at once.

# Mussel Dumpling

**SERVES 4**

*2 lb (1kg) mussels*
*8 oz (225g) self-raising flour*
*4 oz (100g) shredded suet*
*salt and pepper*
*1 small onion*

Prepare the mussels as described in the panel on the right. Remove from their shells and strain the cooking-liquid, keeping on one side. Mix together the flour and suet and season with a pinch of salt. Make into a soft dough with cold water, and use two-thirds of the dough to line a greased 1½ pint (750ml) pudding basin. Put in the mussels, seasoning well with salt and pepper. Add 8 tablespoons cooking-liquid and the finely chopped onion, mixing well. Cover with remaining dough, sealing edges firmly. Cover with greaseproof paper and foil and put into a pan of boiling water. Cover and simmer for 1½ hours, adding more boiling water from time to time to prevent the pan boiling dry. Serve hot with parsley sauce.

Mussels conform to the old rule of 'an R in the month', and they provide great cold-weather food along the North Sea coast. They must be scrubbed and the tough little 'beards' pulled off. If any mussel is open, it must be discarded. Mussels are best cooked in a large covered pan with a little chopped onion and parsley and just enough cider, white wine or apple juice to cover. Over low heat, they will open in just a couple of minutes. They may be eaten at once, with some of the delicious hot liquid, or may be used for the following recipe, formerly cooked in a cloth, but now more easily prepared in a bowl.

**15**

Fresh mussels are popular in the winter months, and in this typical Norfolk recipe they blend with two other famous Norfolk ingredients – cider and mustard.

# MUSSELS IN CIDER SAUCE

**SERVES 4**

*2 lb (1kg) mussels*
*1/4 pint (150ml) dry cider*
*1 teaspoon made wholegrain mustard*
*freshly ground black pepper*
*1 teaspoon cornflour*

If any mussel shell is open, it must be discarded. Scrub the mussels in plenty of cold fresh water and pull away the projecting 'beard'. Put the cider into a large pan and stir in the mustard and pepper. Bring to the boil and put in the mussels. Cover and shake over heat for 3–4 minutes until the mussels have opened. Drain the liquid and reserve.

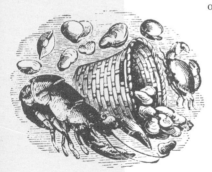

Discard any mussels that have not opened. Remove the rest from their shells and keep on one side.

Put the cooking-liquid into a small pan. Mix the cornflour with 1 tablespoon cooking-liquid and stir into the remaining liquid. Stir over low heat until slightly thickened. Stir in the mussels just enough to heat through. Serve at once with wholemeal or crusty white bread.

Mussels in Cider Sauce

Norfolk beef, lamb and pork have always been excellent. However, the county has been particularly famous for its poultry. Game also abounds, and the long shoreline yields quantities of waterfowl.

This is a delicious way of using birds which are shot on the marsh, but it is equally good made with pheasant, partridge or pigeon, or a mixture of game.

## WILDFOWLER'S PIE

### SERVES 6

*2 wild ducks*
*6 oz (150g) bacon*
*3 oz (75g) butter*
*1 medium onion*
*bay leaf, thyme and parsley*
*1 oz (25g) plain flour*
*³/4 pint (450ml) beef stock*
*¹/2 pint (300ml) red wine*
*12 oz (350g) puff pastry*

Preheat oven to 160°C/325°F/Gas Mark 3. Place the ducks in a roasting-tin. Dice the bacon and cook in a dry pan until crisp. Add half the butter, the finely chopped onion and the herbs and add to the ducks. Roast for 20 minutes, basting occasionally. Pour off fat.

Melt the remaining butter and stir in the flour. Cook until golden brown. Add stock and wine, mix well and bring to the boil. Simmer for 20 minutes. Add duck juices from roasting-tin.

Remove all the meat from the ducks and place in a pie-dish with the onion and bacon. Discard the herbs. Pour over the gravy, and cover with pastry. If liked, brush with a little milk or beaten egg to glaze. Bake at 200°C/400°F/Gas Mark 6 for 40 minutes.

# BROILED PARTRIDGES

## SERVES 4

*2 young partridges*
*1 tablespoon plain flour*
*salt and pepper*
*pinch of Cayenne pepper*
*2 oz (50g) butter*

### Sauce

*2 oz (50g) butter*
*1 oz (25g) plain flour*
*salt and pepper*
*$^1/_2$ pint (300ml) beef stock*
*2 tablespoons mushroom ketchup*

Split the birds in half. Mix the flour with salt, pepper and Cayenne pepper. Coat the partridges lightly with the flour and put them skin-side down in a grill pan without a rack. Grill under high heat for 3 minutes and then turn the birds. Grill for 3 minutes. Melt the butter and brush both sides of the partridge halves. Continue grilling under medium heat, allowing 7 minutes each side and brushing well with butter. Test the birds with a fork. When they are done, they should be tender, and any juice that runs should be colourless. Put on to a warm serving-dish. While the birds are cooking, make the sauce by melting the butter and stirring in the flour. Cook for 1 minute and add seasoning and stock. Stir well and bring to the boil. Simmer for 5 minutes and stir in the mushroom ketchup. Simmer for a further 2 minutes and put into a sauceboat. Serve the partridges with boiled potatoes and a green vegetable.

Norfolk partridge shoots used to be famous, and the plump little birds are a familiar sight, scuttling along hedgerows or across open fields. The small grey partridge is generally thought to have a better flavour than the red-legged or French variety, which is more common. 'Broiled' is the old word for 'grilled', and in the original recipe the birds were cooked over an open fire.

Plough Pudding

# Plough Pudding

**SERVES 6**

*8 oz (225g) self-raising flour*
*4 oz (100g) shredded suet*
*1 lb (450g) pork sausage-meat*
*4 oz (100g) bacon*
*1 large onion*
*2 teaspoons chopped fresh sage*

Mix the flour and suet with a pinch of salt
and enough cold water to make a soft dough.
Roll out and use two-thirds of the dough to
line a greased 2 pint (1 litre) pudding basin.
Press the sausage-meat lightly into the pastry
all round the basin.

Chop the bacon and onion finely and mix
with the sage. Put into the sausage-meat. Add
3 tablespoons water or stock. Cover with the
remaining pastry, pressing the edges together
firmly. Cover with greaseproof paper and foil
and put into a pan of boiling water. Cover
and simmer for 4 hours, adding more boiling
water to the pan from time to time so that it
does not boil dry. Turn the pudding on to a
warm dish and serve with gravy and root
vegetables.

The first Monday
after the Twelve Days
of Christmas was
known as 'Plough
Monday', as it was the
first day of serious
work and winter
ploughing. To make
the day a little more
welcome, there was a
certain amount of
feasting when the
ploughboys and
young men of the
village dressed in
white with horse
brasses, bells and
ribbons, and hauled a
decorated plough
round the village,
accompanied by
mummers or dancers.
Money was collected
to maintain the
Plough Light, lit in the
church on the Sunday
before, when the
farmers and labourers
had their ploughs
blessed and prayers
were offered for a
good harvest. The day
ended with plenty of
ale and a plough
pudding.

# Wild Duck with Port Wine Sauce

## Serves 6

*2 wild ducks*
*2 oz (50g) butter*
*8 rashers streaky bacon*
*salt and pepper*
*pinch of Cayenne pepper*
*juice of 1 lemon*
*4 oz (100g) dark chunky orange marmalade*
*¼ pint (150ml) port*
*½ pint (300ml) beef stock*
*1 teaspoon mushroom ketchup*

On the marshes of North Norfolk wildfowling is a favourite autumn and winter sport. It is a solitary pastime, for a man goes out on the lonely marshes with only a dog for company just before dawn is breaking, and it can be very cold and wet waiting for the birds to come in. This is a good way of cooking the mallard, the largest of the wild ducks, in season from 1 September to the end of February.

Preheat the oven to 200°C/400°F/Gas Mark 6. Truss the birds and prick the skin all over with a fork. Melt the butter and brush it over the ducks. De-rind the bacon and put 4 rashers on each bird. Place in a roasting-tin and roast for 45 minutes.

Remove the bacon and keep on one side. Sprinkle the birds with salt, pepper, Cayenne pepper and lemon juice. Reduce oven to 160°C/325°F/Gas Mark 3. Continue roasting the birds for 10 minutes. Lift them on to a warm serving-dish and garnish with bacon.

Heat the pan juices, scraping all the sediment from the tin and stir in the marmalade, port, stock and ketchup. Simmer for 5 minutes and pour into a sauceboat.

# BRECKLAND RABBIT

## SERVES 6–8

*1 rabbit, jointed*
*2 oz (50g) butter*
*12 cloves*
*1 medium onion*
*12 allspice berries*
*pinch of grated nutmeg*
*³/4 pint (450ml) chicken stock*
*2 teaspoons Worcestershire sauce*
*8 oz (225g) clarified butter*

Soak rabbit joints in cold water for 2 hours.
Drain and dry well, and put into a casserole.
Add 2 oz (50g) butter. Stick cloves into the
onion and add to the casserole with spices
and stock. Cover and cook at 150°C/
300°F/Gas Mark 2 for 3 hours. Cool in the
cooking-liquid for 1 hour.

Remove meat from bones, and mince or
chop finely. Mix with the sauce. Melt 8 oz
(225g) butter and drain off colourless liquid,
leaving the clarified
butter. Add half of
this to the rabbit and
mash well. Moisten
with 4–5
tablespoons
cooking-liquid.
Press into a
straight-sided
dish and cover
with remaining
butter. Chill
until butter is
firm, and serve
with toast.

The rabbit was
introduced to the
scrubby heathlands
known as
'Breckland', where
warreners managed
the sandy acres in a
form of early
intensive farming to
provide fresh meat all
the year round. This
was essential when
cattle and sheep had
to be killed in the
winter because there
was no food for them,
and their meat had to
be salted. The rabbits
bred fast and became
a menace, so the
meat was no longer
cultivated for the
rich, but became
known as 'hollow
meat' to the poor,
who never had
'butcher's meat' until
well after the Second
World War.

Pheasant is in season from 1 October to 1 February. Mushrooms were traditionally gathered from the fields in the early morning mists of October, and here they partner the seasonal pheasant in a dish that is simple to prepare but full of flavour.

# PHEASANT WITH MUSHROOM BUTTER

### SERVES 4

*1 large pheasant*
*8 oz (225g) cap mushrooms*
*3 oz (75g) butter*
*salt and pepper*
*1¹/₂ oz (40g) plain flour*
*³/₄ pint (450ml) chicken stock*
*4 tablespoons dry sherry*

Preheat the oven to 160°C/325°F/Gas Mark 3. Wipe the mushrooms but do not wash or peel them. Slice them thickly. Melt half the butter and cook the mushrooms gently for 10 minutes. Season well with salt and pepper and leave until cool.

Take three-quarters of the mushrooms and stuff the pheasant with them, and truss the bird firmly. Melt the remaining butter and brown the bird all over. Put the pheasant into a casserole.

Work the flour into the pan juices and gradually add the stock. Bring to the boil, stirring well, and simmer until smooth and creamy. Season and pour over the pheasant. Cover and cook for 1¹/₂ hours. Five minutes before serving, stir in remaining mushrooms.

*Pheasant with Mushroom Butter*

# VEGETABLE DISHES

Vegetables flourish in the south of the county, while the rich black soil of the Fens has sustained both salad crops and vegetables. For centuries, vegetables, salads and fruit were not much favoured by country people. Much of the produce was bottled or turned into pickles, while carrots and parsnips were used to sweeten cakes and puddings.

This is a great country favourite made from the dried split peas that were a staple in every house. The pudding was eaten on its own in poor households, but was the ideal accompaniment to pork or bacon dishes.

## PEASE PUDDING

### SERVES 4

*1 lb (450g) split peas*
*salt and pepper*
*1/2 oz (15g) butter*

Put the peas into a clean cloth, leaving them plenty of room to swell, and tie ends of cloth together. Put into cold water, cover and boil until tender, which will take about 2½ hours. Take out of the cloth, sieve and season well. Beat hard with the butter and put into a clean, floured cloth. Tie tightly and boil again for 45 minutes.

A richer pudding used to be made with the addition of 2 beaten eggs and 2 oz (50g) butter or dripping to the sieved peas. For modern times, it is easier to mash the peas with seasoning, chopped onion and butter or dripping, and then bake in a hot oven for 30 minutes.

# CARROTS AND CELERY IN CIDER
### SERVES 4

*1 pint (600ml) dry cider*
*1 lb (450g) carrots*
*1/2 head celery*
*salt and pepper*
*chopped fresh parsley*

Bring the cider to boiling-point. Prepare
the vegetables and cut them into 2 in (5cm)
pieces. Put the carrots into the cider and
simmer gently for 15 minutes. Add celery, salt
and pepper and simmer for 30 minutes. Drain
the vegetables and keep them hot. Boil the
cider until it is reduced to 4 tablespoons. Pour
over the vegetables and sprinkle with parsley.

A delicious mixture
of vegetables with the
county's famous
cider.

# ONION CAKE
### SERVES 4

*1 lb (450g) potatoes*
*10 oz (300g) onions*
*4 oz (100g) butter*
*salt and pepper*

Grease a 7 in (17.5cm) round cake tin with
some of the butter. Peel the potatoes and slice
them fairly thinly. Chop the onions finely.
Starting with a layer of potatoes sprinkled
with onion, build up layers in the prepared
tin, seasoning each onion layer with salt and
pepper, and dotting with flakes of butter.
Finish with a layer of potatoes and a few flakes
of butter. Cover with foil and bake at 180°C/
350°F/Gas Mark 4 for 1 hour. Remove foil
and continue baking for 15 minutes.

This is a useful dish
made from staple
vegetables that were
to be found in every
kitchen. Eat on its
own as a supper dish,
or serve with hot or
cold meat.

# SAMPHIRE

Samphire is a plant that looks like fleshy, green seaweed and grows on the edge of tidal water and marshes (rock samphire is similar but grows on cliffs). In Norfolk, it is at its best during July and August, and it is picked when the tide has washed the plants well. Previously only enjoyed in areas where it grows, samphire is now being served in London restaurants as a garnish to fish and lamb dishes. It is often known as 'St Peter's Cress'.

The roots must be cut from the pieces of samphire and discarded. The fleshy pieces are then washed in fresh water, and boiled in fresh water for 7–10 minutes, to be served with melted butter. The soft flesh is drawn from the spiny stems by the teeth, and for this reason samphire is sometimes called 'poor man's asparagus'.

Samphire may be frozen for winter use, but traditionally it was pickled in sour beer or vinegar, often with a flavouring of ginger and pepper. Often the village baker did the pickling in his oven, as he might be the only person who had one. The samphire was not washed, but left with the sea salt on the surface, then soaked in fresh water with additional salt for 24 hours. It was then drained, covered with malt vinegar and cooked very gently until it came to the boil. The samphire was drained, put into jars and covered with the hot vinegar before sealing. In this way the samphire was kept green and crisp, but the flavour was strong.

# DEREHAM DUCK

## SERVES 4–6

*6 large onions*
*2 cooking-apples*
*1 tablespoon mixed chopped sage and parsley*
*1 oz (25g) fresh breadcrumbs*
*1 tablespoon sugar*
*salt and pepper*
*dripping or butter*

Peel the onions and boil them whole until almost cooked. Drain thoroughly. Place on a flat surface and remove the centre from each. Chop the centres, and put into a bowl. Peel and core the apples, and slice thinly. Mix with the chopped onion centres.

Place the onions in a well-greased baking-dish. Mix the herbs, breadcrumbs, sugar, salt and pepper and stuff the onions, adding one or two small pieces of dripping or butter. Arrange the apple mixture round them and dot liberally with dripping or butter. Cover and bake at 180°C/350°F/Gas Mark 4 for 40 minutes.

It was said in Norfolk that roast duck was once the poor man's dish because there were so many flocks of duck and they were frequently cooked. One farm, however, was recorded as producing this tasty meatless version.

# PUDDINGS

Norfolk is part of the great corn-growing area of East Anglia that boasts the perfect soil and climate for growing wheat and barley. Consequently, traditional puddings tend to be flour-based, either with a suet mixture or with pastry combined with apples grown in the county, and sweetened with treacle, honey or dried fruit.

Apples and suet have always combined well in puddings, and this is a favourite farmhouse dish from the beginning of the 20th century when ovens began to be widely used instead of the earlier open fire. The toffee base turns into a rich sauce during baking.

## BAKED TOFFEE APPLE PUDDING

### SERVES 6

12 oz (350g) plain flour
1 teaspoon baking-powder
6 oz (150g) shredded suet
1 1/2 lb (675g) apples
3 tablespoons dark soft brown sugar

**For the toffee**
2 oz (50g) flaked butter
2 oz (50g) dark soft brown sugar

Make the suet pastry by mixing flour, baking-powder and suet with a little cold water to make a soft dough. Roll out thinly. Grease a pie-dish and sprinkle in brown sugar and flakes of butter. Use about two-thirds of the suet pastry to line the dish.

Peel and core the apples and slice thinly. Put into the pie-dish and sprinkle with 3 tablespoons brown sugar. Cover with the remaining pastry. Bake at 180°C/350°F/ Gas Mark 4 for 1 1/4 hours. Leave to stand for 10 minutes and turn out carefully on to a serving-dish.

*Baked Toffee Apple Pudding*

A 'million' was a kind of marrow which was a common cottage vegetable, and a useful bulk ingredient in the kitchen. Sometimes it was added to a pork pie, or simply cooked with sugar, raisins and water until tender before being covered with a pastry crust and baked. The marrow was considered to be a fruit, rather than a vegetable, so paired naturally with dried fruit. This Norfolk version of the pie omits the fruit but includes jam.

# MILLION PIE

## SERVES 4–6

*8 oz (225g) shortcrust pastry*
*2 oz (50g) jam*
*1 lb (450g) prepared vegetable marrow*
*1 egg*
*2 tablespoons light soft brown sugar*
*pinch of ground nutmeg*

Line a 7 in (17.5cm) round tin with the pastry, saving any trimmings. Spread with a layer of jam. Prepare the marrow by peeling, discarding seeds, and chopping flesh roughly before weighing. Boil the marrow with only a trace of water until soft. Drain well and press out surplus liquid. When cold, beat with the egg, sugar and nutmeg. Put into the pastry case and sprinkle with a little nutmeg. Pastry trimmings may be rolled out and formed into a lattice on the top. Bake at 200°C/400°F/ Gas Mark 6 for 15 minutes. Reduce oven to 180°C/350°F/Gas Mark 4 and continue baking for 10 minutes until golden. Serve hot or cold.

# Norfolk Syllabub

## SERVES 4–6

*1/4 pint (150ml) sweet cider*
*2 tablespoons brandy*
*1 tablespoon sweet sherry*
*1 lemon or Seville orange*
*2 oz (50g) caster sugar*
*1/2 pint (300ml) double cream*

Put cider, brandy and sherry into a large bowl. Peel the lemon or orange very thinly and put the peel into the bowl. Squeeze the juice and strain into the bowl. Stir in the sugar and leave overnight. Take out the peel.

Add the cream and whisk until the mixture forms soft peaks, which will take about 10 minutes (the mixture will splash a great deal). The syllabub should be light and creamy, not like butter. Spoon into 4–6 pretty glasses. Take a small piece of peel and scrape off all the white pith. Cut the peel into very fine shreds and scatter on the syllabub. Keep in a cold place for up to 12 hours.

Syllabub was particularly enjoyed on summer feast-days, and was originally made by milking a cow into a bucket of beer, cider or fruit wine, so that the creamy milk frothed up in the alcohol to produce a foaming rich drink. In the middle of the 18th century, it was found that the addition of acid made the syllabub more solid and long-lasting. Norfolk syllabub is traditionally made from local cider, and it was served in the county's farmhouses on special occasions until the war began in 1939.

*Norfolk Syllabub (previous page) and Norfolk Treacle Tart*

# NORFOLK TREACLE TART

**SERVES 6**

*8 oz (225g) shortcrust pastry*
*4 oz (100g) golden syrup*
*1 oz (25g) unsalted butter*
*grated rind of 1 lemon*
*3 tablespoons double cream*
*1 egg*

Roll out the pastry and line a 7 in (17.5cm) round tin. Prick the base lightly and bake at 200°C/400°F/Gas Mark 6 for 15 minutes. Reduce oven heat to 180°C/350°F/Gas Mark 4.

   Warm the syrup until just runny. Remove from heat and stir in the butter and lemon rind. Beat the cream and egg lightly together and mix into the syrup. Pour into the pastry case. Bake for 30 minutes, and serve just warm or cold with cream.

This delicious dish is sometimes known as 'treacle custard' because it does not contain any breadcrumbs like the traditional treacle tart. It only seems to be made in Norfolk and Suffolk, although the Suffolk version omits the cream. The filling is rich and sets into a light lemon-flavoured jelly, but it is less sweet and filling than the usual recipe. It would originally have been made with black treacle since golden syrup was not invented until the mid-19th century.

*Apple Johns and Biffins*

# APPLE JOHNS

## SERVES 6

*6 large eating-apples*
*6 teaspoons dark soft brown sugar*
*6 teaspoons butter*
*6 cloves*
*12 oz (350g) shortcrust pastry*

Peel the apples and core them. Roll out the pastry and cut into six 6 in (15cm) squares. Put an apple in the centre of each square. Put a spoonful of sugar and butter into each apple and tuck in a clove. Pull up the corners of pastry and pinch them together over each apple. Place on a lightly greased baking-sheet, and brush with milk or egg. Bake at 190°C/375°F/Gas Mark 5 for 30 minutes. Sprinkle with a little caster sugar before serving.

Apple dumplings are always popular, but in Norfolk the apple is paired with crisp baked pastry instead of the solid, boiled plain dough. A good eating-apple that keeps its shape is ideal for this dish, always known as 'Apple Johns' or 'Apple Jacks'. Serve hot or cold, with cream, custard or melted apricot jam.

# BIFFINS

The apples should have no blemishes and should be placed on a layer of clean, fresh straw on a wire cake rack. They must then be covered with another layer of straw before being placed in a very low oven for 5 hours (the cool oven of an Aga is ideal). After this time, they should be gently pressed to flatten them slightly without breaking the skins, then returned to the oven for 1 hour. After gently pressing again, the apples should be left until cold, then coated with sugar that has been melted over a low heat without colouring.

At commercial bakers, the apples were left in the cooling bread ovens for up to 48 hours. They were given to children as a treat, or they could be eaten with cream.

Biffins are a form of baked apple, long-cooked in a slow oven, which used to be sold by Norwich bakers. The apples used were Beaufin, and a similar apple confection was prepared in Normandy. The original Beaufin (or Biffin) still exists in a few gardens, but a Blenheim apple gives a good result.

**37**

# CAKES AND BISCUITS

Sweet foods were special treats, and they were usually simple biscuits that could be easily shaped and cooked in the bread oven as it cooled down. Honey was often used for sweetening, and ginger was the favourite spice. Little biscuits were often known as 'fairings' because they were brought home from fairs on rare holidays.

These biscuits were traditionally eaten at the Tombland Easter Fair in Norwich and at Yarmouth Easter Fair, either in this delicate pale version or richly dark and flavoured with ginger. They were known as 'fairings' along with other sweetmeats and small pieces of china taken home by revellers to those who had not enjoyed a welcome break in the days when Sunday was the only rest day and there were no annual holidays.

## FAIR BUTTONS

*8 oz (225g) plain flour*
*8 oz (225g) caster sugar*
*6 oz (150g) butter*
*1 egg*

Stir together the flour and sugar until evenly mixed. Rub in the butter until the mixture resembles fine breadcrumbs. Beat the egg lightly and work into the mixture. If liked, flavour with a little lemon essence or ground ginger. Roll out thinly and cut into rounds. Bake at 180°C/350°F/Gas Mark 4 for 10 minutes. Lift on to a wire rack to cool.

*Fair Buttons and*
*Norfolk Shortcakes (overleaf)*

Country mothers used to satisfy their children's appetite for sweet foods by wrapping bread dough or pastry round a little lard from the family pig, with a little sugar and dried fruit before baking. In Norfolk, the pastry version was preferred, sometimes using scraps of pastry left over from baking.

# NORFOLK SHORTCAKES

*8 oz (225g) plain flour*
*1/2 teaspoon baking-powder*
*pinch of salt*
*4 oz (100g) lard*
*5 tablespoons water*
*1 1/2 oz (40g) granulated sugar*
*1 1/2 oz (40g) currants*
*caster sugar for sprinkling*

Sieve the flour, baking-powder and salt together. Rub in half the lard until the mixture resembles fine breadcrumbs. Add cold water and mix to a dough. Roll out in a long strip about 1/2 in (1.25cm) thick. Divide the lard, sugar and currants into three portions.

Spread one portion of lard on the pastry and sprinkle with one portion of sugar and one portion of currants. Fold into three layers, and give the pastry a half turn. Roll out lightly and repeat the process twice more. Cut into squares and bake at 200°C/ 400°F/Gas Mark 6 for 15 minutes until golden brown. Sprinkle with caster sugar while hot. Cool and serve freshly baked.

# NELSON SLICES

*8 slices bread (toast thickness)*
*1/2 pint (300ml) milk*
*12 oz (350g) mixed dried fruit*
*2 oz (50g) chopped mixed candied peel*
*1 eating-apple*
*3 tablespoons dark soft brown sugar*
*2 heaped tablespoons marmalade*
*3 tablespoons self-raising flour*
*2 eggs*
*squeeze of lemon juice*
*1 teaspoon ground cinnamon*
*4 oz (100g) butter*
*icing sugar*

This is a Norfolk version of bread pudding, commonly made when every scrap of bread was precious and was recycled in other dishes. It is most commonly eaten as a cake, and is solid, moist and heavy but delicious and sustaining. It is a popular snack with sailors, and was named after Admiral Lord Nelson, a Norfolkman born at Burnham Thorpe.

Grease a 10x14 in (25x35cm) roasting-tin. Preheat oven to 150°C/300°F/Gas Mark 2. Soak the bread, including the crusts, in the milk until soft. Beat in the dried fruit and peel. Peel the apple and grate the flesh into the mixture. Add the sugar, marmalade, flour, eggs, lemon juice and cinnamon. Beat very thoroughly together until the mixture is evenly coloured.

Melt the butter and add half to the mixture. Beat well and put into the prepared tin. Pour on the remaining butter. Bake for 1 hour. Increase heat to 180°C/350°F/Gas Mark 4 and continue baking for 30 minutes. Leave in the tin until cold and sprinkle thickly with sieved icing sugar before cutting into squares.

East Anglia has many historical connections with the Low Countries and Scandinavia, and one reminder of this tradition is the crisp rusk of Norfolk and Suffolk found in no other county. Originally made from bread dough that was baked, split and rebaked, the rusk is now a kind of unsweetened scone which is likewise split and baked. The Suffolk version is smaller and slightly richer, while the Norfolk rusk is plainer, larger and paler. Norfolk rusks were always eaten for breakfast, but are now good with cheese or jam.

# NORFOLK RUSKS

*1 lb (450g) plain flour*
*1 oz (25g) baking-powder*
*pinch of salt*
*5 oz (125g) lard*
*1 egg*
*¹/₄ pint (150ml) milk*

Preheat the oven to 200°C/400°F/Gas Mark 6. Sieve flour, baking-powder and salt. Rub in the lard until the mixture resembles large breadcrumbs. Beat egg and milk together and work into the dry ingredients to make a firm dough. Roll out ¹/₂ in (1.25cm) thick and cut into 2 in (5cm) rounds.

Put on a greased baking-sheet so that they just touch each other. Bake for 15 minutes. While still hot, but cool enough to handle, pull apart (do not cut as the rusks should have a rough surface). Place with cut sides upwards on the baking-sheet. Continue baking for 20 minutes. Cool on a wire rack and store in a tin.

# Norfolk Honey Cake

*2 oz (50g) butter*
*5 oz (125g) clear honey*
*5 oz (125g) demerara sugar*
*10 oz (300g) plain flour*
*pinch of salt*
*1 teaspoon bicarbonate of soda*
*1 teaspoon ground mixed spice*
*1 teaspoon ground ginger*
*1 teaspoon ground cinnamon*
*4 oz (100g) chopped mixed candied peel*
*1 egg*
*1/4 pint (150ml) milk*
*1 oz (25g) flaked almonds*

Grease a 1 lb (450g) loaf tin. Preheat oven to 180°C/350°F/Gas Mark 4. Melt the butter over low heat. Take off the heat and stir in honey and sugar. Mix well and leave until lukewarm. Sift together the flour, salt, soda, spice, ginger and cinnamon, and stir in the peel. Beat the egg and milk together and add to the honey. Pour liquid into the flour and beat until smooth. Pour into the tin and scatter on the almonds lightly. Bake for 1¼ hours. Cool in the tin for 5 minutes and turn on to a wire rack to cool. Serve sliced and buttered.

Sugar was a luxury until the early 18th century, and local honey was used for sweetening all kinds of dishes. It was particularly popular for simple cakes flavoured with spices. Walsingham was especially famous for its bees and for the quality of its honey.

*King Edward's Gingerbread and
Norfolk Honey Cake (previous page)*

# King Edward's Gingerbread

*8 oz (225g) dark soft brown sugar*
*12 oz (350g) black treacle*
*8 oz (225g) butter*
*2 eggs*
*12 oz (350g) plain flour*
*1 oz (25g) ground ginger*
*1 teaspoon lemon juice*
*1 teaspoon bicarbonate of soda*

Preheat oven to 160°C/325°F/Gas Mark 3.
Grease and line an 8 in (20cm) round cake
tin. Mix sugar and treacle in a heavy pan and
heat gently until melted. Cream the butter
and gradually beat in the eggs. Add the
treacle mixture slowly, beating all the time.
Stir ginger into the flour and fold into the
mixture. Stir soda into lemon juice and mix
well. Put into the prepared tin and bake for
1¼ hours. Leave in tin for 10 minutes and
turn on to a wire rack to cool.

King Edward VII
bought Sandringham
House in West
Norfolk in the 19th
century and rebuilt it
as a country retreat.
He loved shooting,
and the estate was
famous for its game.
He also loved
entertaining there,
and the house has
remained a favourite
retreat for the royal
family and their
personal friends. This
rich, golden
gingerbread was
always served to
shooting parties.